MW00744648

Codicil to Will Kit

(United States Edition)

enodare
by Enodare Publishing

Bibliographic Data

- International Standard Book Number (ISBN): 978-1-906144-32-6
- First Printing: May 2011

Published by: Enodare Limited
Unit 102
The Northumberlands
Lower Mount Street
Dublin 2
Ireland

Printed and Distributed By: CreateSpace - An Amazon Company
On-Demand Publishing LLC
Scotts Valley, CA 95066
United States of America

For more information, e-mail books@enodare.com.

Warning and Disclaimer

Although precautions have been taken in the preparation of this kit, neither the publisher nor the author assumes any responsibility for errors or omissions. No warranty of fitness is implied. The information is provided on an "as is" basis. The author and the publisher shall have neither liability nor responsibility to any person or entity with respect to any loss or damages (whether arising by negligence or otherwise) arising from the use of or reliance on the information contained in this kit or from the use of the forms or documents accompanying it.

IMPORTANT NOTE

This kit is meant as a general guide to preparing your own codicil. While considerable effort has been made to make this kit as complete and accurate as possible, laws and their interpretation are constantly changing. As such, you are advised to update this information with your own research and/or counsel and to consult with your personal legal, financial and medical advisors before acting on any information contained in this kit.

The purpose of this kit is to educate and entertain. It is not meant to provide legal, financial or medical advice or to create any attorney-client or advisory relationship. The authors and publisher shall have neither liability (whether in negligence or otherwise) nor responsibility to any person or entity with respect to any loss or damage caused or alleged to be caused directly or indirectly by the information contained in this kit or the use of that information.

This kit may not be suitable for use in Louisiana.

ABOUT ENODARE

Enodare, the international self help legal publisher, was founded in 2000 by lawyers from one of the most prestigious international law firms in the World.

Our aim was simple - to provide access to quality legal information and products at an affordable price.

Our Will Writer software was first published in that year and, following its adaptation to cater for the legal systems of over 30 countries worldwide, quickly drew in excess of 40,000 visitors per month to our website. From this humble start, Enodare has quickly grown to become a leading international estate planning and asset protection self-help publisher with legal titles in the United States, Canada, the United Kingdom, Australia and Ireland.

Our publications provide customers with the confidence and knowledge to help them deal with everyday estate planning issues such as the preparation of a last will and testament, a living trust, a power of attorney, administering an estate and much more.

By providing customers with much needed information and forms, we enable them to place themselves in a position where they can protect both themselves and their families through the use of easy to read legal documents and forward planning techniques.

The Future....

We are always seeking to expand and improve the products and services we offer. However, in order to do this, we need to hear from interested authors and to receive feedback from our customers.

If something isn't clear to you in our publications, please let us know and we'll try to make it clearer in the next edition. If you can't find the answer you want and have a suggestion for an addition to our range, we'll happily look at that too.

USING SELF-HELP KITS

Before using a self-help kit, you need to carefully consider the advantages and disadvantages of doing so – particularly where the subject matter is of a legal or tax related nature.

In writing our self-help kits, we try to provide readers with an overview of the laws in a specific area, as well as some sample documents. While this overview is often general in nature, it provides a good starting point for those wishing to carry out a more detailed review of a topic.

However, unlike an attorney advising a client, we cannot cover every conceivable eventuality that might affect our readers. Within the intended scope of this kit, we can only cover the principal areas in a given topic, and even where we cover these areas, we can still only do so to a moderate extent. To do otherwise would result in the writing of a text book which would be capable of use by legal professionals. This is not what we do.

We try to present useful information and documents that can be used by an average reader with little or no legal knowledge. While our sample documents can be used in the vast majority of cases, everybody's personal circumstances are different. As such, they may not be suitable for everyone. You may have personal circumstances which might impact the effectiveness of these documents or even your desire to use them. The reality is that without engaging an attorney to review your personal circumstances, this risk will always exist. It's for this very reason that you need to consider whether the cost of using a do-it-yourself legal document outweighs the risk that there may be something special about your particular circumstances which might not be taken into account by the sample documents attached to this kit (or indeed any other sample documents).

It goes without saying (we hope) that if you are in any doubt as to whether the documents in this kit are suitable for use in your particular circumstances, you should contact a suitably qualified attorney for advice before using them. Remember the decision to use these documents is yours! We are not advising you in any respect.

In using this kit, you should also take into account the fact that this kit has been written with the purpose of providing a general overview of the laws in the United States. As such, it does not attempt to cover all of the various procedural nuances and specific requirements that may apply from state to state – although we do point some of these out along the way. Rather, in our kit, we try to provide forms which give a fair example of the type of forms which are commonly used in most states. Nevertheless, it remains possible that your state may have specific requirements which have not been taken into account in our forms.

Another thing that you should remember is that the law changes – thousands of new laws are brought into force every day and, by the same token, thousands are repealed or amended every day! As such, it is possible that while you are reading this kit, the law might well have been changed. Let's hope it hasn't but the chance does exist! Needless to say, we take regular steps (including e-mail alerts) to update our customers about any changes to the law. We also ensure that our kits are reviewed and revised regularly to take account of these changes.

Anyway, assuming that all of the above is acceptable to you, let's move on to exploring the topic at hand.........codicils.

TABLE OF CONTENTS

CODICIL TO A LAST WILL AND TESTAMENT

About Codicils

A codicil is a simple document that allows a person to modify some of the provisions in his or her will without the need to draft an entirely new one.

Typically, amendments made by a codicil tend to either add or revoke minor provisions of a will. For example, you may wish to make an amendment to your will because an asset that you had gifted to someone has been sold or because you have acquired a new asset and want to make a gift of that asset to a specific person. However, in other cases, the amendments can completely change the intent of the will such as where the beneficiary of the residuary estate is changed.

Important Note

A "testator" is the name given to someone who has prepared a last will and testament.

In order for a codicil to be deemed valid, it must adhere to the same stringent legal requirements, in terms of composition and signature requirements, as the original will. For this reason, we will have a brief look at wills before moving on to codicils and what you need to do to amend your will.

About Wills

A will, more formally known as a last will and testament, is a legal document that expresses your desires and intentions regarding the distribution of your real and personal property following your death. Real property is generally immovable property such as real estate, homes, land and land improvements. Personal property, on the other hand, includes your movable property such as stocks, bonds, jewelry, furniture, clothing, artwork, etc. Basically, it is your will that determines how, when and even why you want this property apportioned between your relatives, friends and charities. In most cases, your heirs must honor the instructions set out in your will regarding the distribution of your property.

Did You Know?

Historically, a 'will' document was used to transfer real property following a person's death; while a 'testament' document was used only in relation to the disposition of personal property. However, the two documents merged over time to become a single document known as a 'last will and testament'.

In addition to the distribution of your property, your will also appoints one or more people to act as your executor. Your executor will be charged with the task of carrying out the instructions set out in your will and winding up your affairs generally following your death.

Without a will, the decisions as to how your estate will be distributed and who will act as executor will be made by a court in accordance with your state's intestacy laws (i.e. the laws that apply where a person dies without a valid will).

Principal Components of a Will

Standard wills are normally comprised of a number of essential components. These essential components are supplemented and personalized by a number of ancillary clauses that are specific to your own particular circumstances.

Standard wills typically contain the following clauses:

- Preamble* - sets out the name and address of the testator;

- Revocation* – revokes all previous wills and other testamentary documents made by the testator;

- Executor* - appoints a person (or persons) known as an executor(s) (or a personal representative) to wind up the testator's affairs following his or her death;

- Survivorship – a common clause that requires beneficiaries under a will to survive the testator by a fixed period of time, such as 30 days, before they become entitled to inherit under the testator's will. This clause is commonly used in connection with gifts made by one spouse to the other and serves as a means of reducing multiple estate administrations and the possible double payment of estate taxes in respect of the same assets;

- **Cash gift (legacy)** – makes a gift of cash;
- **Specific property gift (bequest)** – makes a gift of a specific item of property;
- **Residue*** - makes a gift of all assets passing through the residuary estate to one or more beneficiaries;
- **Estate administration and expenses** – specifies the means by which the testator's estate is to pay the debts, expenses, taxes and costs of estate administration;
- **UTMA and Child trusts** - creates a type of trust to manage property gifted to minor beneficiaries under the terms of the testator's will;
- **Guardianship** – appoints guardians and successor guardians to care for the testator's minor children;
- **Executive powers*** - sets out the powers to be granted to the executor(s);
- **Executors' fees** – specifies whether the executors should be compensated for their work, or held liable in the event of incurring a loss of estate funds;
- **Attestation*** – the place where the testator signs and executes the will; and
- **Witnessing*** - the place where the witnesses (usually two) sign and attest that they have witnessed the testator sign the will.

*** = these items should appear in every will!**

If you are planning on using a codicil to make a change to your will, you will most likely be amending one of the above components of your will.

Matters That Can Impact Wills

Once a will has been drafted, it's important to remember that there are many events that are likely to occur in your lifetime which will give rise to a need to change the provisions of your will. These events may come around as a result of changes in the law, your financial circumstances, the value of your assets and even in your preferences in relation to beneficiaries. If your will is not updated to address these changes, they can have significant unintended consequences – particularly in respect of the manner in which your assets are ultimately divided amongst your family members.

Some typical changes in circumstances that can cause unintended consequences if not addressed include:

- birth of new family members;
- death of intended beneficiaries;
- significant changes in beneficiaries' circumstances;
- changes in your relationships (such as marriage or divorce);
- acquisition of new assets;
- substantial appreciation in value of particular existing assets; and
- disposal or substantial depreciation in value or loss of certain existing assets.

Important Note

In order to make sure that changes of circumstances are addressed in your will it is recommended that you review and update your will annually or, at the very least, every three years. It's also recommended that you review your will on the occurrence of a significant change in your personal circumstances such as in the cases of the examples set out above.

Updating Your Will

One of the most common ways of updating a will is to simply replace it with a new one. However, where the change is relatively straightforward, many people will use a codicil to avoid the need to re-do the will in full and to avoid the associated cost.

Important Note

Please note that this Codicil is not intended to revoke a will in its entirety.

If you choose to update your will by using a codicil, you need to ensure that it is clearly labeled as a "Codicil" and does not accidentally revoke the provisions of your existing will in full.

Often, when probate courts are confronted with a testamentary document (such as a codicil) that was executed after the date of the original will, they may need to decipher whether the document was intended to be a codicil, or a new will (revoking the terms of the old will in full). Usually, if the second document does not make a complete disposition of the testator's property and does not revoke the original will in its entirety, it will be presumed to be a codicil. That said, you still need to be careful to avoid the risk of accidentally revoking your original will.

In the next section, we have set out a non-exhaustive list of changes that you might wish to make to your will. If you need to make more significant changes than we have provided you with below, you may want to create a new will.

Making Changes to Your Will

When drafting a codicil, it is extremely important that you take the time and care to accurately set out the changes that that you wish to make to your will. These changes should be as clear and detailed as possible. To test your drafting, it may be beneficial to have another person review your proposed changes (before you execute your codicil) to see if they believe that what you have written accurately reflects the changes you want to make to your will.

Codicils tend to have a fairly simple structure. They contain details of your name and address, a recital setting out the reasons why you are making a change to your will and the modification to the will itself. On the assumption that you will have no difficulty with the first element of these details, we will proceed to discuss the recital and modification to the will below.

Recitals to a Codicil

As mentioned, codicils generally include a section which explains why you are making the change to your will. This section is called a 'recital'. While a recital is not necessary to make the codicil valid, it is useful in that it explains the reason the codicil is being made. If the testator explains this reason in a clear and concise manner, the codicil will be more understandable to a judge or others who may be trying to decipher the intent of the testator, after the testator has died.

Here are some common examples of recitals:

Example 1: Following the execution of my Last Will and Testament on [*insert date of execution*], my wife passed away and, on that basis, I am hereby making a redistribution of my gifts, as detailed below.

Example 2: Since the execution of my Last Will and Testament on [insert date of execution], the financial circumstances of my intended beneficiaries have changed and, on that basis, I am hereby making a redistribution of my gifts, as detailed below.

Example 3: For the past number of years, my friend [insert full legal name of friend] has taken care of me and, in recognition of this fact, by this Codicil I hereby give [her/him] [the gifts/the portion of my estate] detailed below.

Example 4: Since the execution of my Last Will and Testament on [insert date of execution], I have acquired and disposed of several assets and, on that basis, I am hereby making a redistribution of my gifts, as detailed below.

Example 5: Since the execution of my Last Will and Testament on [insert date of execution], my sole executor has passed away and, on that basis, I am hereby appointing the two people named below to act as my executors.

Remember, the recitals above only set out the reason why you are making the required change to your Will. The recitals alone <u>are not sufficient</u> to alter your will. You must expressly set out details of the proposed amendment to your will. See section below for more details.

Making Actual Changes to Your Last Will & Testament

Without actually viewing your last will & testament it will not be possible for us to identify the precise changes that you need to make to your will in order to achieve your desired amendments. However, to assist you, we have set out below some common examples of the wording used in codicils to make changes to a last will & testament.

<u>Remember</u>: Make sure your changes easy to read and understand by using simple words and short concise sentences. The real test will be whether a stranger reading your codicil will understand the changes that you have tried to make to your last will and testament.

As there are many reasons for writing a codicil, the examples below are given merely to illustrate the style of writing which may be used in the precedent codicil contained in this kit. Again, remember that you need to adhere to strict legal requirements when making a codicil – these are set out in brief in later sections.

My Last Will & Testament will be modified as follows:

Example 1: *I Direct that [Clause 3] of my Last Will and Testament, dealing with the appointment of executors, is hereby modified by the deletion of the name [insert name] and the insertion of the name [insert name] instead. The name of the alternate executor shall remain the same.*

(OR)

Example 2: *I Direct that [Clause 3] of my Last Will and Testament, dealing with the distribution of my assets following my death, shall be hereby modified to remove the name [insert name] who shall take nothing under my aforementioned Will. I further direct that my daughter [insert name] shall be and is hereby entitled to receive the sum of*

$10,000 out of my estate in addition to any other benefit to which she may be entitled under my said Will.

(OR)

Example 3: *I Direct that [Clause 3] of my Last Will and Testament, which states that at my death my residence located at [insert address] shall go to my spouse, shall be and is hereby changed such that at my death, my residence shall be sold, and the proceeds thereof shall be distributed to the residual beneficiaries of my Will.*

(OR)

Example 4: *I Direct that my daughter, [insert name], who is listed as a beneficiary of one-half of my residuary estate under [Clause 3] of my Last Will and Testament, is hereby expressly disinherited by me from receiving any portion of my estate, and by this directive shall receive nothing from my estate, her portion to be distributed among the remaining residual beneficiaries as set forth in my Will.*

(OR)

Example 5: *That portion of my Will which states that my son, [insert name], is disinherited as a recipient of my estate is hereby revoked in its entirety, and my son, [insert name], shall hereby be entitled to his share of my estate which is shown as being distributed equally to my children.*

Example 6: *[Clause 3] of my Will is hereby revoked and shall be deemed to be deleted in its entirety and all gifts made under [Clause 3] shall for the avoidance of doubt be hereby deemed null and void.*

Example 7: *A new [Clause 7] shall be deemed to be added to my Will and shall read as follows: "I give the sum of $1,000 to my nephew George Shaw of Littlewood, Nevada absolutely".*

The remaining provisions of my Will including the existing [clause 7] shall be deemed to be renumbered accordingly.

Making a Valid Codicil

While most state laws do not expressly provide for a specific format of codicil, all state laws include the minimum elements required for a codicil to be valid. In brief, these are typically the same as the requirements for a will to be valid.

In general, in order for a codicil to be valid, it must:

- be made by a person who has reached the age of majority in his or her state. There are some exceptions to this general rule which we will discuss below;

- be made by a person voluntarily and without pressure from any other person. For this reason, it is not advisable for a potential beneficiary to be present when you prepare your codicil or instruct your lawyer to draw it up or indeed to leave any gifts to anyone who has assisted in the drafting of your codicil;

- be made by a person who is of 'sound and disposing mind';

- be in writing (normally);

- be signed by the testator in the presence of two witnesses or, in the case of codicils executed in the state of Vermont, three witnesses;

- be signed by all the witnesses in the presence of the testator (after he or she has signed it) and in the presence of each other. A beneficiary under the codicil or the spouse or registered partner of such a beneficiary should not act as a witness to the signing of the codicil. If such a beneficiary or the spouse or registered partner of such a beneficiary act as a witness, the gift to the beneficiary under the codicil shall be deemed to be invalid, although the codicil itself will remain valid;

- include an attestation clause; and

- be notarized if made in the state of Louisiana.

Age of Majority

The age of majority is a legal description that denotes the threshold age at which a person ceases to be a minor and subsequently becomes legally responsible for his or her own actions and decisions. It is the age at which the responsibility of the minor's parents or guardians over the minor is relinquished. Reaching the age of majority also has a number of important practical consequences for the minor. The minor is now legally entitled to do certain things which he or she could not legally do before. For example, he or she is now legally entitled to enter into binding contracts, hold significant assets, buy stocks and shares, vote in elections, buy and/or consume alcohol, and so on. But more importantly from an estate planning perspective, the minor can now make a will and a codicil.

It is a general rule in each state that a person must reach the age of majority in their home state before being entitled to make a valid legal will or codicil. There are however some exceptions to this general rule. Typically, a person under the age of majority who is already married, or who has been married, is deemed of sufficient age to execute a will or a codicil. Emancipated minors may also execute a will or a codicil. An underage person who joins the military or is on active military service can also make a will or a codicil, as can a seaman or naval officer at sea.

Lastly, and in addition to the above, a court can specifically authorize the making of a will or codicil by a minor on application by the minor's parents or guardians. This might be approved, for example, where a minor inherited a large amount of money, invented some innovative computer software or created the next 'You Tube' with some friends. In each case, if the minor is shown to be of a sound disposing capability and the move is deemed prudent, the court will usually consider granting approval for the making of a will or codicil by the minor.

Mental Capacity and Undue Influence

In order to make a valid legal codicil, you must typically be of sound and disposing mind and memory. While what constitutes being of 'sound and disposing mind and memory' differs slightly from state to state, it is generally taken to mean someone who understands:

- what a codicil is;
- that they are making a codicil;
- the general extent of their property;
- who their heirs and family members are; and
- the way in which their codicil proposes to distribute their property (and, of

course, to be satisfied with that).

It is important to note that you need to be of sound mind and memory when you execute your codicil, not immediately prior to your death. As such, if you end up suffering from any kind of mental impairment late in life such as dementia or Alzheimer's disease, or even from an addiction to drugs or alcohol, the court will look at your mental state at the time you executed your codicil in order to determine whether it was validly made. If it can be shown that you were not mentally impaired or under the influence at the time you executed your codicil, the court will most likely deem the codicil to be valid. If you are suffering from any such impairments, it is advisable that you visit your doctor on the day you execute your codicil (or even execute it in your doctor's presence) and have your doctor prepare a medical certificate stating that in his or her professional opinion you were mentally competent and lucid at the time you executed your codicil. These types of statements generally have a strong persuasive effect on the courts, which typically tend to concede mental lucidity in such cases.

Another form of mental incapacity comes under the heading 'undue influence'. Undue influence is the exertion by a third party in a position of trust or authority of any kind of control or influence over another person such that the other person signs a contract or other legal instrument (such as a mortgage or deed) which, absent the influence of the third party, he or she would not ordinarily have signed. A contract or legal instrument (such as a will) may be set aside as being non-binding on any party who signs it while under undue influence.

Claims of undue influence are often raised by sibling beneficiaries in circumstances where one sibling is bequeathed more from a parent than the others. In making your codicil, you must therefore be careful to avoid potential claims of undue influence where you leave more to one of your children that another. Any such suggestion would give an aggrieved beneficiary the opportunity to attack and try to overturn the terms of your codicil. In order to reduce the potential likelihood of such claims, it's often useful to document the reasons why you are leaving more to one child than another. Your note can then be attached to your will or codicil or at least kept with them.

A second scenario in which claims for undue influence are often raised arises where a testator uses a beneficiary's attorney to draft their will or codicil. In such circumstances, aggrieved beneficiaries will, in reliance on that very fact, often assert that the use of the beneficiary's lawyer was evidence of the control the beneficiary had over the testator and the pressure that the beneficiary put on the testator to make the provisions he or she did in the codicil.

Example

John constantly visits his uncle Bryan, an 88 year old retired business tycoon, in the nursing home. During his visits, John continuously urges Bryan to leave his vast business interests to him – to the detriment of Bryan's own children who don't visit as often as they should. John, knowing that Bryan is lonely and depressed, threatens to stop visiting him as he is clearly ungrateful for John's kindness and attention. John finally arrives at the nursing home with his lawyer, who has never met Bryan before. John remains present while Bryan instructs the lawyer to write a new codicil for him in which he purports to leave all his business interest's to John.

Ideally, an ethical attorney should never agree to make a will or codicil in such circumstances, but, in reality, it does happen. Therefore it's always wise to get independent legal advice when you make a will or codicil.

Executing a Codicil

State laws set out the formal requirements for executing a codicil. While these laws (which are similar to those which apply to wills) are fairly similar in each state, you should still check the specific requirements applicable in your state. In general, however, a 'best practice' guide for executing your codicil could be summarized as follows:-

- while it is only a legal requirement in the State of Louisiana, you should write your initials, in the presence of two witnesses (in Vermont, you should have three witnesses), at the bottom of each page of your codicil, except the last (signature) page;

- each of the witnesses should then, in your presence and in the presence of each other, initial each page next to where you just placed your initials;

- you should then insert the date on which you are signing the codicil in the space provided on the final page of the codicil;

- you should write your initials beside where you inserted the date;

- each of the witnesses should then, in your presence and in the presence of each other, write their initials beside where you placed your initials (i.e. beside the date);

- you must then sign your ordinary signature, using a pen, in the space provided on the final page; and

- each witness must then, in your presence and in the presence of each other, write his/her name and address in the space provided on the final page of the codicil and then sign their name with their normal signature.

While the actual execution of your codicil should be relatively straightforward, there are a number of additional rules which you need to be aware of when executing your codicil. These rules relate specifically to witnesses and notarization.

In relation to witnesses firstly, they should be at least 18 years of age or older and should not be your spouse, partner or a beneficiary under your codicil (or a spouse or registered partner of such beneficiary), as this could invalidate any gifts made to them thereunder.

Only in the State of Louisiana must a will or codicil be notarized. In all other states notarization is not required — however it is recommended.

Finally, once you have executed your codicil, remember to keep it in a safe place. You should also consider informing your executor or even a close family member or friend of the location of your codicil so that it can be located when needed.

Important Note

Generally, a codicil must be signed by you or by someone directed to do so on your behalf. Signatures may include marks, initials, a rubber stamp, a 'nick-name' or even a former name.

APPENDIX 1

SIGNING INSTRUCTIONS

Instructions For Completion of The Codicil Document

Carefully read all the instructions below.

1. Carefully edit the text version of the form (that is available to you to download) on your computer.

2. In the first paragraph, (i) insert your name and address, (ii) specify whether this is the first, second, third etc codicil to your will and (iii) insert the date of your original will.

3. In clause 1, you will need to complete the recital. Use the examples contained in this kit to help you draft an appropriate recital. Remember, if you are unsure of the wording that you are using, you can always ask a third party (who is neither a beneficiary under your codicil or a witness to its execution) to review the wording.

4. In clause 2, you will need to specify the changes that you wish to make to your original will. Use the examples contained in this kit to help you draft the appropriate amendments. Remember, if you are unsure of the wording that you are using, you can always ask a third party (who is neither a beneficiary under your codicil or a witness to its execution) to review the wording.

5. While it is only a legal requirement in the State of Louisiana, you should write your initials, in the presence of two witnesses (in Vermont, you must have three witnesses), at the bottom right hand corner of each page, except the last page. Each of the two witnesses (or three as the case may be) should then initial each page next to where you placed your initials.

6. You must then insert the date on which you signed the codicil in the space provided on the final page. (e.g. 1st day of January 2011).

7. You should write your initials beside where you inserted the date. Each of the witnesses must then place their initials beside where you placed your initials.

8. You must then sign your ordinary signature, using a pen, in the space provided on the final page above the word "(Signed)".

9. The witnesses must then, in your presence, insert the date on which they witnessed you sign the codicil and then write his/her name and address in the space provided at the end of the codicil; and then sign with their normal signature.

10. The witnesses should be at least 18 years of age or older.

11. A witness should not be your spouse or a beneficiary under your codicil as this could serve to invalidate any gift made to them under the codicil.

12. Only in the State of Louisiana must a codicil or will be notarized. In all other states notarization is not required - however it is recommended.

13. The codicil should be placed with your will.

Resource

Legalvaults.com is an online storage facility which enables you to store your important documents securely online. You may also make certain documents (such as enduring powers of attorney and living wills) and important medical information available to close family members in case of an emergency. To find out more about the services offered by legalvaults, visit their website at www.legalvaults.com.

APPENDIX 2

SAMPLE CODICIL

Disclaimer — The following "Codicil" form is a basic form. It is not intended to be and is not legal advice. Read it carefully and decide for yourself if it meets your needs. If you have any questions whatsoever, talk with a lawyer licensed in your state. This is a 'do-it-yourself" document and you alone are responsible for its construction and execution.

Downloadable Forms

Blank copies of this form are available to download from our website.

Web: http://www.enodare.com/downloadarea/

Unlock Code: COD98764

enodare

CODICIL

I *[full name]* of *[address]* DECLARE this to be a *[first/second/etc]* Codicil to my Will dated *[insert date of Will]*:

1. [Insert Recital].

2. [Insert proposed change(s)].

3. In all other respects I confirm my said Will and any other Codicils thereto.

IN WITNESS HEREOF, I sign the foregoing as my Codicil to my Last Will and Testament, do it willingly and as my free and voluntary act for the purpose herein expressed, this ____ day of ____________ 201__.

____

(Signed)

Signed by the above-named as and for his/her Codicil in our presence, both of us being present at the same time who at his/her request and in his/her presence and in the presence of each other have hereunto subscribed our names as witnesses.

We, the witnesses, sign our name to this document, and we declare under penalty of perjury, that the foregoing is true and correct, this ________ day of ________________, 20__.

Name: ______________________________

Signature: ______________________________

Address: ______________________________

____

____

____

Name: ______________________________

Signature: ______________________________

Address: ______________________________

____

____

____

[Delete signature block below if not needed]

Name: ______________________________

Signature: ______________________________

Address: ______________________________

____

____

____

APPENDIX 3

WILL WRITING WORKSHEET

WILL WRITING WORKSHEET

WILL WRITTING WORKSHEET

Before you begin the process of making a will or codicil, we recommend that you print out this worksheet and complete it as appropriate. It will help you to work out what assets you actually own, and identify your liabilities, before deciding who you would like to make gifts to and how. By having all the relevant details at your fingertips it will save a considerable amount of time in the preparation of your estate planning documents.

The document is also useful for documenting your choice of fiduciaries such as executors, trustees, healthcare agents etc.

In addition, by keeping this worksheet with your will and other personal papers, it will greatly assist your executor in identifying and locating your assets and liabilities when the time comes.

Personal Information	**You**	**Your Spouse**
Full Name:		
Birth Date:		
Social Security Number:		
Occupation:		
Work Telephone:		
Work Fax:		
Mobile/Pager:		
Email Address:		
Home Address (Include State):		
Home Telephone:		
Home Fax:		
Date and Place of Marriage:		
Maiden Name of Spouse:		
If either of you were previously married, list the dates of prior marriage, name of previous spouse, names of living children from prior marriage(s), and state whether marriage ended by death or divorce:		
Location of Safe Deposit Box (if any):		

Notification of Death

(On my death, please notify the following persons)

Full Name	Telephone	Address

Children *(Living)*

Full Name	Address (If child does not reside with you)	Birth Date

Children *(Deceased)*

Full Name		

Grandchildren

Full Name	Address	Birth Date

Parents

Full Name	Address	Telephone Number

Brothers and Sisters

Full Name	Address	Telephone Number

Assets

Description & Location	Current Fair Market Value	How is Title Held?
Real Estate (Land and Buildings)		
Closely Held Companies, Businesses, Partnerships etc.		
Bank Accounts		

Shares, Bonds and Mutual Funds		
Vehicles, Boats, etc		
Other Property		
Total		

Liabilities

Description	Amount
Mortgages	
Loans	

Debts	
Other Liabilities	
Total	

Life Insurance and Annuities

Company	Insured	Beneficiary(ies)	Face Amount	Cash Value
Total				

Pensions and Other Retirement Plans

Company Custodian	Participant	Type of Plan	Vested Amount	Death Benefit
Total				

Distribution Plan (Describe in general terms how you wish to leave your property at death)

Other Beneficiaries

(Information about persons other than your spouse and family members who you wish to benefit)

Full Name	Age	Address	Relationship to You

Fiduciaries
(List name, address and home telephone for each person)

	Full Name	**Address**	**Telephone Number**
Last Will and Testament			
Primary Executor:			
First Alternate Executor:			
Second Alternate Executor:			
Primary Trustee:			
First Alternate Trustee:			
Second Alternate Trustee:			
Guardian of Minor Children:			
First Alternate Guardian:			
Second Alternate Guardian:			
Family Trust			
Successor Trustee:			
First Alternate Successor Trustee:			
Second Alternate Successor Trustee:			
Agent under a Power of Attorney for Finance and Property (Enduring Power of Attorney)			
Agent:			
First Alternate Agent:			
Second Alternate Agent:			
Agent under a Healthcare Power of Attorney (Healthcare)			
Healthcare Agent:			
First Alternate Healthcare Agent:			

Second Alternate Healthcare Agent:			
Living Will			
Healthcare Agent:			
First Alternate Healthcare Agent:			
Second Alternate Healthcare Agent:			

Advisors (List name, address and home telephone for each person)			
	Full Name	**Address**	**Telephone Number**
Lawyer			
Accountant			
Financial Advisor			
Stockbroker			
Insurance Agent			
Other Information:			

Document Locations		
Description	**Location**	**Other Information**
Last Will & Testament		
Trust Agreement		
Living Will		
Healthcare Power of Attorney		
Power of Attorney for Finance and Property		
Title Deeds		
Leases		
Share Certificates		

Mortgage Documents		
Birth Certificate		
Marriage Certificate		
Divorce Decree		
Donor Cards		
Other Documents		

Funeral Plan (Describe in general terms what funeral and burial arrangements you would like to have)

Other Great Books from Enodare's Estate Planning Series

Make Your Own Medical & Financial Powers of Attorney

The importance of having powers of attorney is often underappreciated. They allow people you trust to manage your property and financial affairs during periods in which you are incapacitated; as well as make medical decisions on your behalf based on the instructions in your power of attorney document. This ensures that your affairs don't go unmanaged and you don't receive any unwanted medical treatments.

This book provides all the necessary documents and step-by-step instructions to make a power of attorney to cover virtually any situation!

Make Your Own Living Trust & Avoid Probate

Living trusts are used to distribute a person's assets after they die in a manner that avoids the costs, delays and publicity of probate. They also cater for the management of property during periods of incapacity.

This book will guide you step-by-step through the process of creating your very own living trust, transferring assets to your living trust and subsequently managing those assets.

All relevant forms are included.

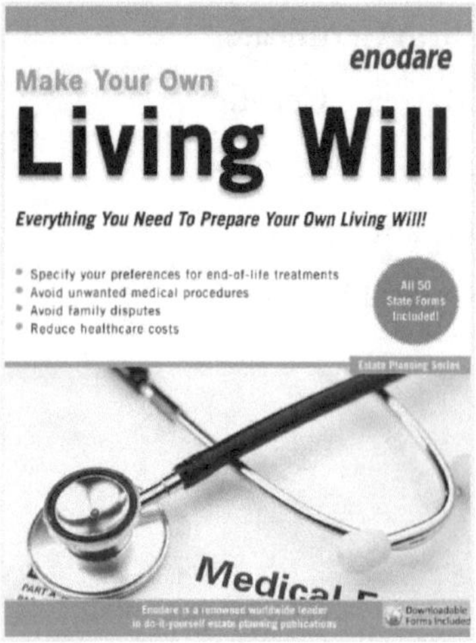

Make Your Own Living Will

Do you want a say in what life sustaining medical treatments you receive during periods in which you are incapacitated and either in a permanent state of unconsciousness or suffering from a terminal illness? Well if so, you must have a living will!

This book will introduce you to living wills, the types of medical procedures that they cover, the matters that you need to consider when making them and, of course, provide you with all the relevant forms you need to make your own living will!

www.enodare.com

Other Great Books from Enodare's Estate Planning Series

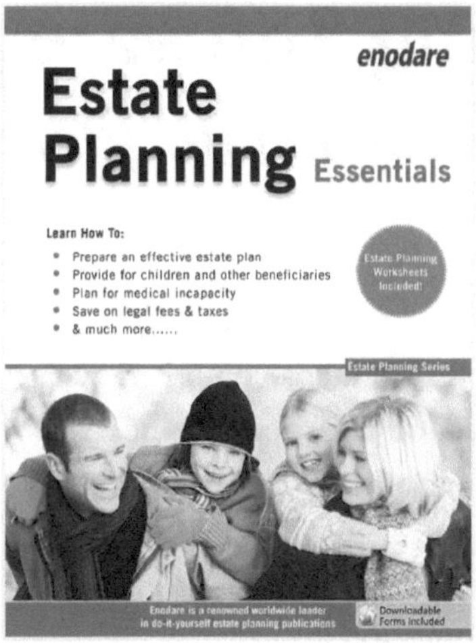

Estate Planning Essentials

This book is a must read for anyone who doesn't already have a comprehensive estate plan.

It will show you the importance of having wills, trusts, powers of attorney and living wills in your estate plan. You will learn about the probate process, why people are so keen to avoid it and lots of simple methods you can actually use to do so. You will learn about reducing estate taxes and how best to provide for young beneficiaries and children.

This book is a great way to get you started on the way to making your own estate plan.

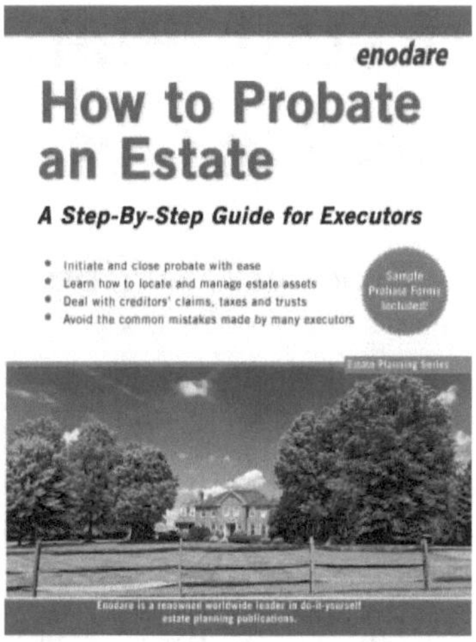

How to Probate an Estate - A Step-By-Step Guide for Executors

This book is essential reading for anyone contemplating acting as an executor of someone's estate!

Learn about the various stages of probate and what an executor needs to do at each stage to successfully navigate his way through to closing the estate and distributing the deceased's assets.

You will learn how an executor initiates probate, locates and manages assets, deals with debt and taxes, distributes assets, and much more. This is a fantastic step-by-step guide through the entire process!

Funeral Planning Basics - A Step-By-Step Guide to Funeral Planning

Through proper funeral planning, you can ensure that your loved ones are not confronted with the unnecessary burden of having to plan a funeral at a time which is already very traumatic for them.

This book will introduce you to issues such as organ donations, purchasing caskets, cremation, burial, purchasing grave plots, organization of funeral services, legal and financial issues, costs of pre-arranging a funeral, how to save money on funerals, how to finance funerals and much more.

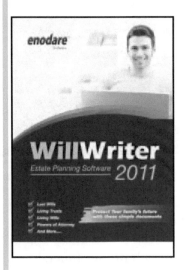

Ensure Your Family's Protected

Healthcare Power of Attorney

Appoint someone you trust to make medical decisions for you if you become mentally incapacitated.

Power of Attorney for Finance and Property

Appoint someone you trust to manage your financial affairs if you become mentally incapacitated, or if you are unable to do so for any reason.

And More.........

Enodare's Will Writer software also includes documents such as self proving Affidavits, Deeds of Assignment, Certifications of Trust, Estate Planning Worksheet, Revocation forms and more.

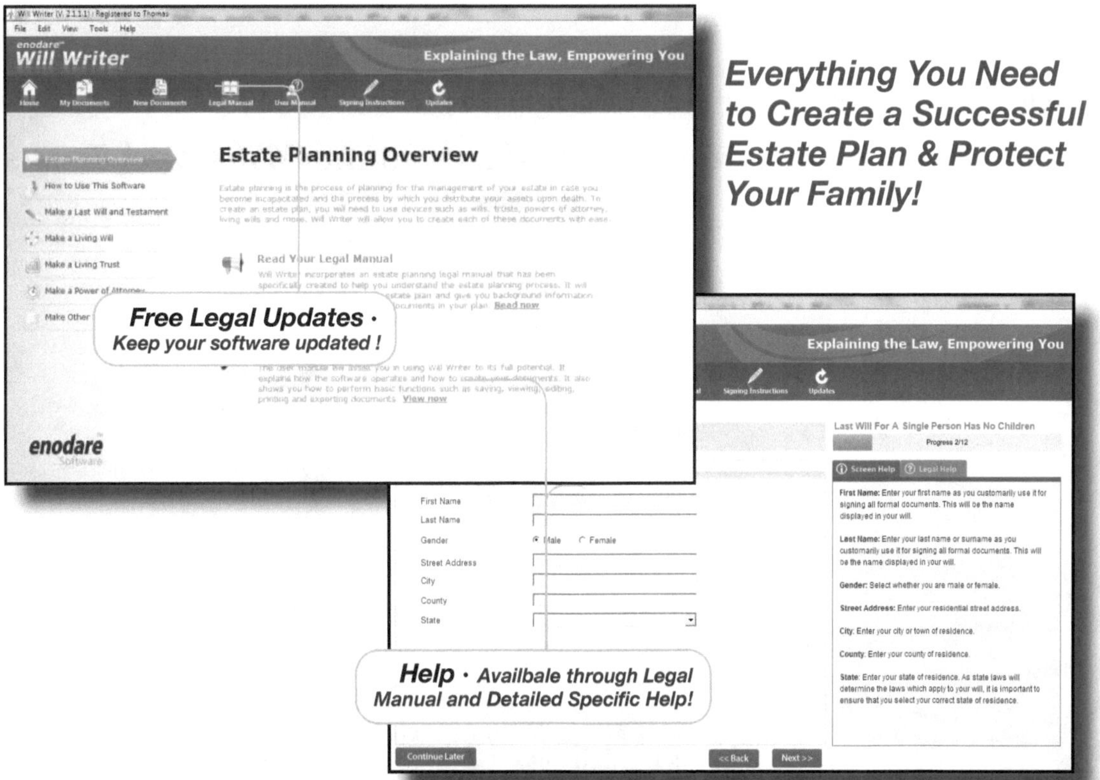

Everything You Need to Create a Successful Estate Plan & Protect Your Family!

www.enodare.com

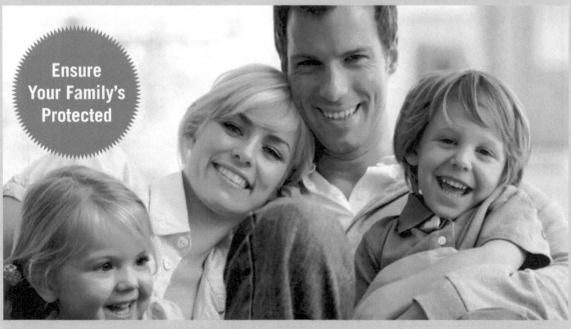

Made in United States
Troutdale, OR
11/03/2023

14281153R00027